Emergency Hallelujah

To John —

Hope you enjoy the book.

All the best,

Jason Heroux

Emergency Hallelujah

Jason Heroux

Mansfield Press

Library and Archives Canada Cataloguing in Publication

Heroux, Jason, 1971-
    Emergency hallelujah / Jason Heroux.

Poems.

ISBN 978-1-894469-40-1

    I. Title.

PS8565.E825E44 2008   C811'.54   C2008-905892-5

Editor for the Press: Stuart Ross

Design: Mansfield Creative

Cover Photo: iStockphoto

The publication of *Emergency Hallelujah* has been generously supported by
the Canada Council for the Arts and
the Ontario Arts Council.

Mansfield Press Inc.

25 Mansfield Avenue, Toronto, Ontario, Canada M6J 2A9

Publisher: Denis De Klerck

www.mansfieldpress.net

For my father and mother
Robert Heroux and Marina Leichner
My brother Darren
And Soheir

Contents

Old Neighbourhood

In the old neighbourhood
I lived above a clothing store
that was always going

out of business.
Tall naked mannequins
kept borrowing my sugar.

The paperboy was
an elderly blind woman.
She always called me sweetie

and still blows me kisses
every morning
though I've been gone for years.

Sunday in San Pietro Infine

I woke up this morning
in a strangely tender mood
as if I were a mushroom

that had sprouted between
the third and fourth steps
of an old wooden staircase.

We're in a small cold house
on the hillside: the hot water
tank and the electrical heaters
can't run at the same time
or the fuse box blows.

But it's like that outside too.
Not a lot happens here at once
or everything switches off.

The dog doesn't bark
when the rooster crows,
and the trees only blossom
when no one is watching.

A Heavy Snowplow Is Clearing the Roads

There is a sorrow in the world no one owns.
It is dark and early, a quiet Sunday morning.
The snow has fallen where it doesn't belong.
And a heavy snowplow is clearing the roads.

Yesterday

Yesterday
a yellow pear
sat on the table.

Today it is gone.

But I still recall
its skin

the colour
of a curtain drawn
across the window

of a very tiny room.

Winter Vista

These short winter mornings.
The early hours when
the clocks have little to do

leaning against the walls
with fidgety hands.

I glance outside
and see bare
winter trees

empty as jail cells
with their doors hanging open

and the sun
broken down and
stripped for parts.

In the parking lot
a man brushes a crisp
white sheet of snow off

his cold car as if identifying
a body at the morgue

and the houses by the side
of the road all stare
in the same direction:

faces in an elevator
avoiding each other.

These short
winter mornings,
early hours when

the sad-eyed houses
look tired of always
being outdoors

and cars hurry through
the streets like insects
with only three days to live.

Midwinter

In midwinter the heart
cleans graffiti from its walls
and trees in the forest

tremble like old twisted
forklifts loading and unloading
dark packages of crows.

The city sidewalks
are ashtrays overflowing
with crushed footprints

and cold dead leaves
sway in the wind like
empty swings in the playground.

Next Door

My next-door neighbour is dying next door.
He doesn't have the strength
to carry his garbage once a week to the curb.
He leaves it on the porch and leaves the porch light on.
Once a week I carry it for him to the curb with my own.

It's almost light enough for me to carry with no hands.
How little and light it is. It saddens me
four times a month to see how little garbage the dying have.
I carry it to the curb with no hands, it's almost light enough.
The porch light shines through the night until it shuts off.

The Trees Are Very Still

The trees are very still
and handling the moonlight
carefully, as if it were a loaded gun
that could go off at any moment.
I fell asleep on my couch
listening to evening's dark music
on the window's radio.
Somewhere scientists
are working day and night to invent
sex and violence suitable for all ages.

The Dog Woke Up

The dog woke up and stretched his legs. But I'm not a dog, the dog
said. I'm a human being. The dog took a shower, ate some breakfast,
and drove to work. Please stop calling me a dog, the dog said. You're
giving people the wrong impression — it's not fair. After work
the dog drove home, watched some television, and then prepared
dinner. Listen, whoever you are, for the last time, I'm not a dog, the
dog said, and looked a little sad. The dog started to cry. But I'm not
even crying. This is ridiculous, the dog said, with tears in his eyes.

Rue de la Quarantine

The other day the sun
broke its tooth

on a tough
speck of dust.

A dead mailman
stumbled
from house to house
delivering handfuls of dirt

and rain puddles
glistened
in the grass

like expired mirrors
slowly lowered down
into little graves.

In the Backyard

In the backyard
an impoverished
stone grips its shadow

like a dark lottery ticket
before the draw.

At dusk a handful
of startled stars
bark in the sky

just before all
the others join in.

I look at my wristwatch
and see the arms
moving up and down,

the empty sleeves
of a shirt on the line
swaying in a slow breeze.

The grass is starting to return
from a journey
it no longer remembers,

blades slanted like the masts
of miniature boats in a vast marina.

Insomnia

The seconds
jump like
grasshoppers
in the clock's field

and the birds are quiet
cash registers in a store
that hasn't yet opened.

Our dreams wait nearby,
motionless cars
with keys locked inside.

We lie awake
listening to the wind
grip the dark window

as if trying to open a jar
of frightened black jam.

One Day the Sun Fell

One day the sun fell down
and the clouds looked warm and
flushed like they'd been drinking.
The trees wandered into town
searching for food because the forest
wasn't where it was anymore.
I shot one with my gun
and it just stopped
and stood still
dying for a thousand years.

Shoes

It started raining shoes, all sorts of shoes: tennis sneakers, bedroom slippers, loafers, and even jackboots. Who did they belong to? There were so many in the street we were drowning in them. We couldn't wear them all. People began burying the shoes. I tried to find the ones that matched and put them together. The mayor called a town meeting. "It's just a dream," he told everyone. They passed a law that said we had to shake each other to make sure we were all awake. Only criminals slept. And the shoes kept falling.

On the Outskirts of Desire

The fallen snow swallows
the small dark pills
of our footprints.
We're tired of seeing
the dead kill themselves
over and over again
in Iraq while the rich
fuck each other with
crisp hundred dollar bills.
Our televisions are dying
of cancer, lying awake
at night in the hospital
watching each other.
The winter trees have
blown their brains out.
The poor sewer rats
need psychiatric help.
The snow-covered cars
in the snow-covered parking lot
are massive blank headstones
in a massive blank graveyard.

Codeine

The moonlight shines on the wall
showing blank slides
of vacations it never went on.

Talking About the War

As we sat outside after dinner one evening
talking about which colours to paint
the rooms of our house, it suddenly seemed
we were really talking about the war.

The trees rustled, the sky grew dark,
and the full moon glowed with a powerless light.
We sat outside for a while longer and said nothing at all
and it still seemed we were talking about the war.

The Dead Are My Neighbours

The dead are my neighbours
and their dogs never bark.
In the winter they water
my grass when I'm gone.
In the summer they remove
the snow from my car.
Brushing it clean
like a large white
tooth before bed.

The Sea Never Drowns

Clouds in the sky don't know they're clouds.
Stones in the path go wherever they're kicked.
I don't expect to win prizes for being myself.

The traffic driving home sounds like the traffic
heading out, and the chimney smoke's
pale waterfall flows upward.

Sometimes a rusted bolt blurts out the truth:
we have work we don't even know about.
We get paid every time we take a breath.

There is a sorrow stuck in us
like a house unable to pass through its door.
Although it can't swim, the sea never drowns.

I like hearing noisy trucks celebrate
the uneven road but I also enjoy,
when the traffic has gone,
the sound of the road on its own.

Three Notes Toward an Elegy

I

A light rain falls, leaving
spots on the sidewalk:
the heads of nails
hammered all the way in.

2

Outside a crowded funeral
home the hearse glides away
down an empty street
with Stop signs in full bloom.

3

All day we drift
in a daze, lightheaded
as curtains quivering
near an open window.

Postcard from a Parking Lot

We're having a wonderful time.
It's so quiet and peaceful.
The summer dust silently
drifts through the late
evening light like coins

in an out-of-order jukebox.
Last night we saw an army
of ants scurry over the ragged
hillside of a half-eaten apple.
And tomorrow we're setting out

on a long journey just to hear
our shoes click against
the pavement like forks
scraping around
the bottom of a jar.

The Administration Spent Millions

The administration spent millions
designing a better, more efficient
stone that could do in one day
what it took other stones a week to do.
I spend millions gazing through a window.
Meanwhile the sky is broke and wearing
second-hand clothes and begging for enough
money to use a pay toilet — it can't
go to the bathroom with everyone watching.

Thrift Shop

A thrift shop in a seedy part of town with drug-addicted mannequins in the window. The rats keep nibbling on their plastic toes. Autumn leaves blow in each time someone opens the door. The discounted nightgowns hover on the rack. They look like souls made of silk, souls shivering in moonlight with easy-to-wash instructions. "This isn't my real life," the salesgirl assures me. I stand there nodding my head. It's not my real life either. Outside over the rooftops the moon hangs in the sky like a silver medal, as if the world won second prize in a contest.

The Morning Light

The morning light
embraces what is
out in the open, it never
shines in people's pockets.
It clings to the cobwebs

and the suspension bridge.
It clings to the merchandise
in the shop window and
the broken pieces of glass
in the alley, waking us up

before we have a chance
to remember our names.
The morning light knocks
shadows to the ground:
long dark fence posts

blown down by a storm.
And we're like upright roads
that have risen from the world
but still have that trampled feeling
of everyone hurrying over us.

No Swimming Allowed

There is no swimming allowed
in the public library
though not a single sign says so.
The police are giving tickets
to trees that stand too still.
I don't understand all the details.
It's a bright winter afternoon
and the sun has already started moving
its furniture out of the day's apartment.

There Is a Law Against

There is a law against everything
even eating powdered cheese puffs
in a powdered cheese puff factory.
That's why I wrote you
a three-page love letter disguised
as an overdue phone bill.
It helps me sleep at night knowing
there is a law against the moon washing
its dirty white hair in our drinking water.

Flower Shop

An old woman
pushing a stroller
paused in front
of a flower shop.
She stood on her
own dark shadow
as if it were a bridge
she was afraid to cross.
I'm not sure what
went through her mind.
She put on her gloves
— a chill gripped the air —
and continued on her way.
All this happened years ago.
The flower shop is now torn
down and the woman is gone.
I watched her disappear around
the corner and then closed my eyes.
I'm not sure what went through my mind.

Hotel Room

The hotel furniture looks tired
and worn-out as salmon

swimming against the current
of an irreversible evening light.

A skyscraper's shadow
crashes to the ground:

an oak tree unable
to support its own weight.

There's so much more to this
world than just life and death.

The seagulls soar over the city rooftops:
white sails that have escaped their boats.

The Fallen Snow Pauses

The fallen snow pauses
on the tree branch
like a train
at the second-
to-last station.

I Desire a Normal World

I desire a normal world
full of normal
atomic bombs
to make us feel safe
at night when we're dead.

The Hospital

We return our overdue pain
so others may
borrow it for a while.
The hospital is a library where
everyone is allowed
to scream as loud as they want.

Cityscape

In the evening the wealthy sun
shines through all the windows
like a presidential speech on every channel.

The streetlamp clicks on in the quiet sky:
an ice cube dropped into an empty glass.

You look down and see a cigarette butt
smouldering as if someone's dinner
is burning inside.

You look up and see the part-time sky
has gone to its other job to make ends meet.

Lost Forest

A small forest
walking through us
has lost its way.
It can't find the path it was on.
It's been missing for centuries
and it's starting to grow weak
waiting for the search party.
Some of the leaves have raindrops
pinned to them like transparent name tags.
We should find the leaves before they forget about us.
Every evening in the city, clocks eat from their troughs
and our shadows lengthen in the street
like dark receipts from a concrete cash register.
As if this life can be returned to the store for another.
But there is no other life. There is barely this one.
We feel the lost forest inside us closing its eyes.
A sorrow belonging to everyone floats through air
like graffiti without a wall.

Night of Light Rain

Raindrops with empty fuel tanks
gather on a tree branch and wait

like cars at a gas station.
Our souls turn off their engines.

The grass rows back and forth
in wind: oars without boats.

Suicidal Toaster

The toaster grew quiet and moody, keeping to itself. Whenever I
put bread in it, the toaster popped up too early, as if it didn't care
about bread anymore. Something was wrong. It used to love toasting
bread. One day I came home to a strange smell. Dark smoke filled
the kitchen, and an empty bottle of sleeping pills sat on the counter.
I turned the toaster upside-down and shook out as many burnt pills
as I could, then rushed it to the hospital. The doctors said the toaster
was lucky this time; another few minutes and it would've been
too late. I brought the toaster home. "Talk to me," I said. "Tell me
what's wrong. I want to help." But the toaster didn't say anything.
When I woke up the next day, the toaster had thrown itself through
a window and smashed into pieces on the sidewalk below. It didn't
even leave a note behind. Just a few crumbs scattered on the counter,
which I keep reading over and over, trying to make sense of it all.

On This Street

In the morning
the mirror glows
like a brush after
grooming the sun.

At night it wanders off,
a dark horse unhitched
from the room's wagon.

On this street the houses
are fussy eaters.
Windows spit out the light
and feed it
to the dog under the table.

The tiny stars
reflected in puddles
look dirty as vitamins
fallen under the fridge.

Unemployed trees
pick their own pockets.
Statues with stomach ulcers
cough up other people's blood.

On this street it's hard to tell
if it's day or night.

When it gets dark
the light bulbs hatch
in the lampshade's nest
and cry until they're fed.

Potato

Never in my wildest dreams
did I hope to be a person in this life.
I didn't even know what a person was
until I became one.
That's how ignorant I was.
I wanted to be a potato
to be honest with you
a hard-working potato
with a brilliant
future.

In the Sane Asylum

In the sane asylum the inmates say please
and thank you, and we're allowed
to shave with sharp razors.
Out in the real world normal people
eat handfuls of dirt and
the President thinks he's a bicycle.
He sleeps chained to a street lamp
so that no one steals him
in the middle of the night.

The Apple

The apple was fine. It was the orange I worried about. The orange was broken and acting strange. I could hear something rattling around inside it. The repairman said it would take months to get replacement parts. I tried to nurse the broken orange back to health, but the poor orange wasn't in its right mind, and I was afraid it might do something dangerous. It started rolling wildly on the floor as if in great pain. At night I heard it crying quietly to itself. Although I'd just purchased the orange last week I felt I'd known it my whole life. We were like brothers. I brought it to a specialist who told me the orange was beyond repair. "Even the replacement parts won't help it now," he said. I didn't know what to do. I felt helpless watching the orange suffer. But the apple was fine. There was nothing wrong with the apple.

All the Streets Are Empty

All the streets are empty.
The moon is a white orange.
I hear you in the kitchen
chopping something
against a cutting board.
No, that's not true:
I don't hear you at all.
All I hear is the knife
against the cutting board.

Sunday

Sunday is made in China once a week.
It is guaranteed to last all day.
If it breaks you can always bring it back.

If it coughs up blood
they will replace the parts.
The church bells yell

at the top of their lungs
and everything is always closed.
The stores forget what stores are for.

The sun's medication makes the moon
bloated and drowsy and the sky
overdoses operating heavy machinery.

Five O'Clock

Five o'clock, late February.
The evening light
is learning a new language.

Wounded smoke
limps from the
chimney's hospital.
The clocks operate
on a dying hour.

The moon pins
itself to the sky

a silver name tag
that says: Hello,
My Name Is Tonight.

A last bit of daylight
shoots through the window's veins.

Today

Today arrived
on a trembling crutch
of birdsong looking
for someplace to rest.

It carried the sky
under its arm

like a broken suitcase
tied shut with a string
of chimney smoke.

Remember

Don't forget the bright summer afternoons:
the clock hands picking the hour's pockets,
last year, a decade ago, in another lifetime,

the insect-bitten leaves full of holes
like magazines with recipes cut out,
the patio umbrella's shade

dark as the inside of a medieval church.
Don't forget the flies
buzzing in air

like small bridges
humming with traffic.
Remember the sluggish wind chime

that never made a sound.
Remember the weightless joy
sitting on the butcher's empty scale.

It Wasn't Early or Late

It wasn't early or late
but still I was tired.
I set the alarm clock to go off
right at this moment
but it didn't help.
All I heard was the graffiti
of a crow's voice
spray-painted across the sky.
The only other sound was the wind
screaming that its purse was stolen.

Octoberland

The trees were empty and we shook hands with the fallen leaves,
greeting them while bidding ourselves farewell.

The clouds overhead looked like crumpled suicide notes.
Our neighbours walked around solemnly hosing their lawns,
burying the dead water deep in the ground.

The poor grass kept growing like a sweater knit by the dirt.
The cobwebs swayed in air like yesterday's chimney smoke.
At night the mushrooms flickered like miniature streetlamps
and the neon signs glowed with words no one ever spoke.

Evening Hour

It's the evening hour even though
the streetlamps aren't on yet,

and the day feels like it may never end.

It's the evening hour;
the spider moves feverishly

in her web, a deckhand rigging the sails,
and the shadows

appear bloated and swollen
as if stung by bees. It's the evening hour

though the stores are all still open

and no one is hurrying home.
There is the feeling this life will never end.

But it's evening because the light is dusty
as hair on a barbershop floor and the roads

are returning from places they've never been.

Odd-Sized Screws Kept in a Drawer

The traffic sparkles under the sun, cameras
flashing at a family reunion. The world
drains the window's glass in one long gulp.
Grasstrumpets sway in the earth's orchestra.

The clock ticks, clearing stones from a field.
We cling to life like chimney smoke
above the dark rooftops of our shadows.
We'll die and get put aside for a while

like odd-sized screws kept in a drawer.
Even if we never get used for anything again
it'll feel okay to stretch out freely for once.
It'll feel okay holding nothing together.

Living Forever for a Little While

I

A warm October morning after a night of rain,
a sleepy autumn wind milks dead leaves from the tree
while the clock hands dig through the hour's soft dirt.

We hear the city's excited sidewalks
bark with footsteps, and the sound of ants
pushing the small dark shopping carts of their shadows.
The sun knocks on the locked doors of each leaf
as the wet blades of grass sway back and forth,
windshield wipers during a storm.

The sunlight's plant grows in the window's soil.
The autumn trees lean their ladders against the invisible,
ladders the earth tries to climb up
while the sky tries to climb down.

The leaves tremble in the wind,
telephones ringing with wrong numbers,
and the clouds wake up stretching with light.
The clock ticks like someone knocking
against his own door when he's not home.
Our lives are short but infinitely wide.

The autumn leaves are rags that soak up
something that can't be wrung out.
Everyone lives forever for a little while.

The day doesn't know what day it is.
A traffic jam of dead flies
sits bumper to bumper
in the cobweb's streets.

The leaves are thin and worn
as the elbows of second-hand shirts
and the stones throw their shadows
like last night's coffee onto the grass.

In the afternoon quiet birdsongs flow
through air like blood without a wound
and bees are little cans of spray paint
leaving invisible graffiti on the flowers.

The sun takes a few steps and then stops
in its tracks as if tangled up in a leash.
I watch the after-rain drip from the trees
and hear the leaves cough
with autumn's smoke in their lungs.

The crumpled leaves have faces
but they all look the same, the faces
of people we look away from, the poor,
the sick, those we pretend not to see.

Some of them whisper brief prayers of wind
shivering like blankets too small to cover themselves,
some stumble across the grass like bruised moths,
some are pitched like little tents to keep
their homeless shadows warm through the night.

The sunlight's snail crawls in a shell of cloud.
Its antennas touch the afternoon's soul
then feel their way back
across a cobweb's broken bridge.

Meanwhile the clocks build nests
of straw-like seconds as daylight's music
plays faintly through the window's radio
and ringing church bells bark with fear.

The grass blades kneel
in the dark cathedrals of each other's shadows
and leaves fall like a flight of stairs without steps.

3

In the afternoon the sky starts to lose its voice,
and all our shadows are made of the same dark fabric.

The wind sounds like it's driving home after work
and the fallen leaves appear crumpled and creased
as if they lived and died stuffed in someone's pockets.

The stones listen quietly to each other
while the distant bridge breathes with unseen traffic
and a handful of grass blades share a single shiver
passing it back and forth all day.

The grey afternoon cloud-light is the colour of ash.
Transparent thumbtacks
of rain keep the light attached to the sky.
Transparent thumbtacks of pain
and happiness keep us attached to ourselves.

4

Late in the evening the sun sheds its leaves,
and the light is tucked into sparkling beds
of broken glass in the parking lot.

The evening hatches from a window's egg
and steam rises up through the sewer grates
like earth piled around an anthill.

The light's razor rusts in the sky's drawer.
The streetlamps quietly milk themselves
as dusk gathers at the window, a clump
of hair brushed from a smoke-coloured cat.

Autumn leaves shiver in their sleepless sleep,
desolate and abandoned
as the train stations of towns where no one lives.

The window brushes the moon's long white voice
and a train of endless wind travels through the trees.

5

The evening light
locks itself
in the window's vault
for safekeeping

but still gets stolen each night.
Something inside us feels sad
as rain that hasn't fallen
all the way to earth

and the dying sky creeps like music
further and further from its instrument.
The autumn leaves are lampshades
aching for their lights to turn off

and ants hurry back and forth
like small black ambulances without a hospital.

There is always something cheering and booing in us
as if the soul scored a winning goal against itself.
The faint moon glows bare as an empty hospital bed.
The earth eats the fake fingernails of fallen leaves

while the windows darken like tree bark in rain.
The air's rusted machinery is starting to fall apart.
The little engines of bees are running out of gas,
hovering near the flowers
like old keys after the locks have been changed.

Leaves on the tree rustle sad as footsteps
that have never walked on the ground.
The wind's pen runs out of ink in the grass.
The shadows are so thin you can see their bones.
The moonlight is fragile as an egg without a shell.

6

In the middle of the night when
the sky isn't home, the sun's voice leaves
a message on the moon's answering machine.

Sometimes we feel piled up outside ourselves
like the mail of someone who moved away, and our hearts
limp inside us as if they have one leg longer than the other
while the dark trees count their leaves like cashiers
balancing their registers at the end of the shift.

Night is the time when footsteps lose their voice,
when stones forget what they were about to say next,
when a drop of water weighs more than its weight.

The moon's reflection hatches like an egg
in the rain puddle's nest
and the dark headlight of a stone's shadow
shines on the earth.

Acknowledgements

Some of these poems previously appeared in the magazines
*Alba, Arc, Exile Quarterly, The Haight-Ashbury Literary Review, The
Malahat Review, Microbe Revue, My Favorite Bullet, Sein und Werden,
Street, This Magazine,* and *Zone,* and in the chapbooks *Unfinished
Elephant* (In Case of Emergency Press, 2006), *Renovation in the
House of Mirrors* (Mercutio Press, 2007), *The Sea Never Drowns*
(Sunnyoutside, 2007), and *Black Coffee* (Old World Booklets, 2008).

"The Morning Light" and "Evening Hour" appeared as broadsides
printed by Sunnyoutside and Big Tree Press, respectively. Many
thanks to Tim Conley and Clelia Scala, Ben Kalman, David Michael
McNamara, Glen Downie, Stuart Ross, Michael Glover, and John
Francis Phillimore.

Jason Heroux is the author of *Memoirs of an Alias* (2004). His work has appeared in chapbooks, anthologies and magazines in Canada, the U.S., Belgium, France, and Italy. He lives in Kingston, Ontario, with Soheir Jamani.